We did this to ourselves

· ·

· ·

This is one of our last days of freedom

/   /

Doom's Day

/   /

Guests

I'm so happy you're having a baby and I'm not!

....

Um...Now what do we do?

....

....

Wishes For The Lil Poop Factory

....

....

Baby's First Swear Word

....

Who will hit the bottle first?

....

Willing to babysit? (Please, we're begging you)

....

Guests

I'm so happy you're having a baby and I'm not!

....

Um...Now what do we do?

....

....

Wishes For The Lil Poop Factory

....

....

Baby's First Swear Word

....

Who will hit the bottle first?

....

Willing to babysit? (Please, we're begging you)

....

Guests

I'm so happy you're having a baby and I'm not!

....

Um...Now what do we do?

....

....

Wishes For The Lil Poop Factory

....

....

Baby's First Swear Word

....

....

Who will hit the bottle first?

....

....

Willing to babysit? (Please, we're begging you)

....

Guests

I'm so happy you're having a baby and I'm not!

....

Um...Now what do we do?

....

....

Wishes For The Lil Poop Factory

....

....

Baby's First Swear Word

....

Who will hit the bottle first?

....

Willing to babysit? (Please, we're begging you)

....

Guests

I'm so happy you're having a baby and I'm not!

....

Um...Now what do we do?

....

....

Wishes For The Lil Poop Factory

....

....

Baby's First Swear Word

....

....

Who will hit the bottle first?

....

....

Willing to babysit? (Please, we're begging you)

....

Guests

I'm so happy you're having a baby and I'm not!

....

Um...Now what do we do?

....

....

Wishes For The Lil Poop Factory

....

....

Baby's First Swear Word

....

....

Who will hit the bottle first?

....

Willing to babysit? (Please, we're begging you)

....

Guests

I'm so happy you're having a baby and I'm not!

....

Um...Now what do we do?

....

....

Wishes For The Lil Poop Factory

....

....

Baby's First Swear Word

....

Who will hit the bottle first?

....

Willing to babysit? (Please, we're begging you)

....

Guests

I'm so happy you're having a baby and I'm not!

....

Um...Now what do we do?

....

....

Wishes For The Lil Poop Factory

....

....

Baby's First Swear Word

....

....

Who will hit the bottle first?

....

....

Willing to babysit? (Please, we're begging you)

....

Guests

I'm so happy you're having a baby and I'm not!

....

Um...Now what do we do?

....

....

Wishes For The Lil Poop Factory

....

....

Baby's First Swear Word

....

Who will hit the bottle first?

....

Willing to babysit? (Please, we're begging you)

....

Guests

I'm so happy you're having a baby and I'm not!

....

Um...Now what do we do?

....

....

Wishes For The Lil Poop Factory

....

....

Baby's First Swear Word

....

Who will hit the bottle first?

....

Willing to babysit? (Please, we're begging you)

....

Guests

I'm so happy you're having a baby and I'm not!

....

Um...Now what do we do?

....

....

Wishes For The Lil Poop Factory

....

....

Baby's First Swear Word

....

Who will hit the bottle first?

....

Willing to babysit? (Please, we're begging you)

....

Guests

I'm so happy you're having a baby and I'm not!

....

Um...Now what do we do?

....

....

Wishes For The Lil Poop Factory

....

....

Baby's First Swear Word

....

....

Who will hit the bottle first?

....

Willing to babysit? (Please, we're begging you)

....

Guests

I'm so happy you're having a baby and I'm not!

....

Um...Now what do we do?

....

....

Wishes For The Lil Poop Factory

....

....

Baby's First Swear Word

....

....

Who will hit the bottle first?

....

....

Willing to babysit? (Please, we're begging you)

....

Guests

I'm so happy you're having a baby and I'm not!

....

Um...Now what do we do?

....

....

Wishes For The Lil Poop Factory

....

....

Baby's First Swear Word

....

....

Who will hit the bottle first?

....

....

Willing to babysit? (Please, we're begging you)

....

Guests

I'm so happy you're having a baby and I'm not!

....

Um...Now what do we do?

....

....

Wishes For The Lil Poop Factory

....

....

Baby's First Swear Word

....

Who will hit the bottle first?

....

Willing to babysit? (Please, we're begging you)

....

Guests

I'm so happy you're having a baby and I'm not!

....

Um...Now what do we do?

....

....

Wishes For The Lil Poop Factory

....

....

Baby's First Swear Word

....

Who will hit the bottle first?

....

Willing to babysit? (Please, we're begging you)

....

Guests

I'm so happy you're having a baby and I'm not!

....

Um...Now what do we do?

....

....

Wishes For The Lil Poop Factory

....

....

Baby's First Swear Word

....

Who will hit the bottle first?

....

Willing to babysit? (Please, we're begging you)

....

Guests

I'm so happy you're having a baby and I'm not!

....

Um...Now what do we do?

....

....

Wishes For The Lil Poop Factory

....

....

Baby's First Swear Word

....

Who will hit the bottle first?

....

Willing to babysit? (Please, we're begging you)

....

Guests

I'm so happy you're having a baby and I'm not!

....

Um...Now what do we do?

....

....

Wishes For The Lil Poop Factory

....

....

Baby's First Swear Word

....

....

Who will hit the bottle first?

....

....

Willing to babysit? (Please, we're begging you)

....

Guests

I'm so happy you're having a baby and I'm not!

....

Um...Now what do we do?

....

....

Wishes For The Lil Poop Factory

....

....

Baby's First Swear Word

....

Who will hit the bottle first?

....

Willing to babysit? (Please, we're begging you)

....

Guests

I'm so happy you're having a baby and I'm not!

....

Um...Now what do we do?

....

....

Wishes For The Lil Poop Factory

....

....

Baby's First Swear Word

....

....

Who will hit the bottle first?

....

....

Willing to babysit? (Please, we're begging you)

....

Guests

I'm so happy you're having a baby and I'm not!

....

Um...Now what do we do?

....

....

Wishes For The Lil Poop Factory

....

....

Baby's First Swear Word

....

....

Who will hit the bottle first?

....

....

Willing to babysit? (Please, we're begging you)

....

Guests

I'm so happy you're having a baby and I'm not!

....

Um...Now what do we do?

....

....

Wishes For The Lil Poop Factory

....

....

Baby's First Swear Word

....

....

Who will hit the bottle first?

....

....

Willing to babysit? (Please, we're begging you)

....

Guests

I'm so happy you're having a baby and I'm not!

....

Um...Now what do we do?

....

....

Wishes For The Lil Poop Factory

....

....

Baby's First Swear Word

....

Who will hit the bottle first?

....

Willing to babysit? (Please, we're begging you)

....

Guests

I'm so happy you're having a baby and I'm not!

....

Um...Now what do we do?

....

....

Wishes For The Lil Poop Factory

....

....

Baby's First Swear Word

....

....

Who will hit the bottle first?

....

Willing to babysit? (Please, we're begging you)

....

Guests

I'm so happy you're having a baby and I'm not!

....

Um...Now what do we do?

....

....

Wishes For The Lil Poop Factory

....

....

Baby's First Swear Word

....

Who will hit the bottle first?

....

Willing to babysit? (Please, we're begging you)

....

Guests

I'm so happy you're having a baby and I'm not!

....

Um...Now what do we do?

....

....

Wishes For The Lil Poop Factory

....

....

Baby's First Swear Word

....

Who will hit the bottle first?

....

Willing to babysit? (Please, we're begging you)

....

Guests

I'm so happy you're having a baby and I'm not!

....

Um...Now what do we do?

....

....

Wishes For The Lil Poop Factory

....

....

Baby's First Swear Word

....

Who will hit the bottle first?

....

Willing to babysit? (Please, we're begging you)

....

Guests

I'm so happy you're having a baby and I'm not!

....

Um...Now what do we do?

....

....

Wishes For The Lil Poop Factory

....

....

Baby's First Swear Word

....

Who will hit the bottle first?

....

Willing to babysit? (Please, we're begging you)

....

Guests

I'm so happy you're having a baby and I'm not!

....

Um...Now what do we do?

....

....

Wishes For The Lil Poop Factory

....

....

Baby's First Swear Word

....

....

Who will hit the bottle first?

....

Willing to babysit? (Please, we're begging you)

....

Guests

I'm so happy you're having a baby and I'm not!

....

Um...Now what do we do?

....

....

Wishes For The Lil Poop Factory

....

....

Baby's First Swear Word

....

Who will hit the bottle first?

....

Willing to babysit? (Please, we're begging you)

....

Guests

I'm so happy you're having a baby and I'm not!

....

Um...Now what do we do?

....

....

Wishes For The Lil Poop Factory

....

....

Baby's First Swear Word

....

Who will hit the bottle first?

....

Willing to babysit? (Please, we're begging you)

....

Guests

I'm so happy you're having a baby and I'm not!

....

Um...Now what do we do?

....

....

Wishes For The Lil Poop Factory

....

....

Baby's First Swear Word

....

....

Who will hit the bottle first?

....

....

Willing to babysit? (Please, we're begging you)

....

Guests

I'm so happy you're having a baby and I'm not!

....

Um...Now what do we do?

....

....

Wishes For The Lil Poop Factory

....

....

Baby's First Swear Word

....

Who will hit the bottle first?

....

Willing to babysit? (Please, we're begging you)

....

Guests

I'm so happy you're having a baby and I'm not!

....

Um...Now what do we do?

....

....

Wishes For The Lil Poop Factory

....

....

Baby's First Swear Word

....

Who will hit the bottle first?

....

Willing to babysit? (Please, we're begging you)

....

Guests

I'm so happy you're having a baby and I'm not!

....

Um...Now what do we do?

....

....

Wishes For The Lil Poop Factory

....

....

Baby's First Swear Word

....

Who will hit the bottle first?

....

Willing to babysit? (Please, we're begging you)

....

Guests

I'm so happy you're having a baby and I'm not!

....

Um...Now what do we do?

....

....

Wishes For The Lil Poop Factory

....

....

Baby's First Swear Word

....

Who will hit the bottle first?

....

Willing to babysit? (Please, we're begging you)

....

Guests

I'm so happy you're having a baby and I'm not!

....

Um...Now what do we do?

....

....

Wishes For The Lil Poop Factory

....

....

Baby's First Swear Word

....

Who will hit the bottle first?

....

Willing to babysit? (Please, we're begging you)

....

Guests

I'm so happy you're having a baby and I'm not!

....

Um...Now what do we do?

....

....

Wishes For The Lil Poop Factory

....

....

Baby's First Swear Word

....

....

Who will hit the bottle first?

....

Willing to babysit? (Please, we're begging you)

....

Guests

I'm so happy you're having a baby and I'm not!

....

Um...Now what do we do?

....

....

Wishes For The Lil Poop Factory

....

....

Baby's First Swear Word

....

Who will hit the bottle first?

....

Willing to babysit? (Please, we're begging you)

....

Guests

I'm so happy you're having a baby and I'm not!

....

Um...Now what do we do?

....

....

Wishes For The Lil Poop Factory

....

....

Baby's First Swear Word

....

....

Who will hit the bottle first?

....

Willing to babysit? (Please, we're begging you)

....

Guests

I'm so happy you're having a baby and I'm not!

....

Um...Now what do we do?

....

....

Wishes For The Lil Poop Factory

....

....

Baby's First Swear Word

....

....

Who will hit the bottle first?

....

Willing to babysit? (Please, we're begging you)

....

Guests

I'm so happy you're having a baby and I'm not!

....

Um...Now what do we do?

....

....

Wishes For The Lil Poop Factory

....

....

Baby's First Swear Word

....

Who will hit the bottle first?

....

Willing to babysit? (Please, we're begging you)

....

Guests

I'm so happy you're having a baby and I'm not!

....

Um...Now what do we do?

....

....

Wishes For The Lil Poop Factory

....

....

Baby's First Swear Word

....

....

Who will hit the bottle first?

....

Willing to babysit? (Please, we're begging you)

....

Guests

I'm so happy you're having a baby and I'm not!

....

Um...Now what do we do?

....

....

Wishes For The Lil Poop Factory

....

....

Baby's First Swear Word

....

Who will hit the bottle first?

....

Willing to babysit? (Please, we're begging you)

....

Guests

I'm so happy you're having a baby and I'm not!

....

Um...Now what do we do?

....

....

Wishes For The Lil Poop Factory

....

....

Baby's First Swear Word

....

....

Who will hit the bottle first?

....

Willing to babysit? (Please, we're begging you)

....

Guests

I'm so happy you're having a baby and I'm not!

....

Um...Now what do we do?

....

....

Wishes For The Lil Poop Factory

....

....

Baby's First Swear Word

....

....

Who will hit the bottle first?

....

....

Willing to babysit? (Please, we're begging you)

....

Guests

I'm so happy you're having a baby and I'm not!

....

Um...Now what do we do?

....

....

Wishes For The Lil Poop Factory

....

....

Baby's First Swear Word

....

....

Who will hit the bottle first?

....

Willing to babysit? (Please, we're begging you)

....

Guests

I'm so happy you're having a baby and I'm not!

....

Um...Now what do we do?

....

....

Wishes For The Lil Poop Factory

....

....

Baby's First Swear Word

....

Who will hit the bottle first?

....

Willing to babysit? (Please, we're begging you)

....

Guests

I'm so happy you're having a baby and I'm not!

....

Um...Now what do we do?

....

....

Wishes For The Lil Poop Factory

....

....

Baby's First Swear Word

....

Who will hit the bottle first?

....

Willing to babysit? (Please, we're begging you)

....

Guests

I'm so happy you're having a baby and I'm not!

....

Um...Now what do we do?

....

....

Wishes For The Lil Poop Factory

....

....

Baby's First Swear Word

....

Who will hit the bottle first?

....

Willing to babysit? (Please, we're begging you)

....

Guests

I'm so happy you're having a baby and I'm not!

....

Um...Now what do we do?

....

....

Wishes For The Lil Poop Factory

....

....

Baby's First Swear Word

....

Who will hit the bottle first?

....

Willing to babysit? (Please, we're begging you)

....

Guests

I'm so happy you're having a baby and I'm not!

....

Um...Now what do we do?

....

....

Wishes For The Lil Poop Factory

....

....

Baby's First Swear Word

....

....

Who will hit the bottle first?

....

....

Willing to babysit? (Please, we're begging you)

....

Guests

I'm so happy you're having a baby and I'm not!

....

Um...Now what do we do?

....

....

Wishes For The Lil Poop Factory

....

....

Baby's First Swear Word

....

Who will hit the bottle first?

....

Willing to babysit? (Please, we're begging you)

....

Guests

I'm so happy you're having a baby and I'm not!

....

Um...Now what do we do?

....

....

Wishes For The Lil Poop Factory

....

....

Baby's First Swear Word

....

Who will hit the bottle first?

....

Willing to babysit? (Please, we're begging you)

....

Guests

I'm so happy you're having a baby and I'm not!

....

Um...Now what do we do?

....

....

Wishes For The Lil Poop Factory

....

....

Baby's First Swear Word

....

Who will hit the bottle first?

....

Willing to babysit? (Please, we're begging you)

....

Guests

I'm so happy you're having a baby and I'm not!

....

Um...Now what do we do?

....

....

Wishes For The Lil Poop Factory

....

....

Baby's First Swear Word

....

....

Who will hit the bottle first?

....

Willing to babysit? (Please, we're begging you)

....

Guests

I'm so happy you're having a baby and I'm not!

....

Um...Now what do we do?

....

....

Wishes For The Lil Poop Factory

....

....

Baby's First Swear Word

....

Who will hit the bottle first?

....

Willing to babysit? (Please, we're begging you)

....

Guests

I'm so happy you're having a baby and I'm not!

....

Um...Now what do we do?

....

....

Wishes For The Lil Poop Factory

....

....

Baby's First Swear Word

....

....

Who will hit the bottle first?

....

Willing to babysit? (Please, we're begging you)

....

Guests

I'm so happy you're having a baby and I'm not!

....

Um...Now what do we do?

....

....

Wishes For The Lil Poop Factory

....

....

Baby's First Swear Word

....

Who will hit the bottle first?

....

Willing to babysit? (Please, we're begging you)

....

Guests

I'm so happy you're having a baby and I'm not!

....

Um...Now what do we do?

....

....

Wishes For The Lil Poop Factory

....

....

Baby's First Swear Word

....

Who will hit the bottle first?

....

Willing to babysit? (Please, we're begging you)

....

Guests

I'm so happy you're having a baby and I'm not!

....

Um...Now what do we do?

....

....

Wishes For The Lil Poop Factory

....

....

Baby's First Swear Word

....

Who will hit the bottle first?

....

Willing to babysit? (Please, we're begging you)

....

Guests

I'm so happy you're having a baby and I'm not!

....

Um...Now what do we do?

....

....

Wishes For The Lil Poop Factory

....

....

Baby's First Swear Word

....

Who will hit the bottle first?

....

Willing to babysit? (Please, we're begging you)

....

Guests

I'm so happy you're having a baby and I'm not!

....

Um...Now what do we do?

....

....

Wishes For The Lil Poop Factory

....

....

Baby's First Swear Word

....

Who will hit the bottle first?

....

Willing to babysit? (Please, we're begging you)

....

Guests

I'm so happy you're having a baby and I'm not!

....

Um...Now what do we do?

....

....

Wishes For The Lil Poop Factory

....

....

Baby's First Swear Word

....

Who will hit the bottle first?

....

Willing to babysit? (Please, we're begging you)

....

Guests

I'm so happy you're having a baby and I'm not!

....

Um...Now what do we do?

....

....

Wishes For The Lil Poop Factory

....

....

Baby's First Swear Word

....

Who will hit the bottle first?

....

Willing to babysit? (Please, we're begging you)

....

Guests

I'm so happy you're having a baby and I'm not!

....

Um...Now what do we do?

....

....

Wishes For The Lil Poop Factory

....

....

Baby's First Swear Word

....

Who will hit the bottle first?

....

Willing to babysit? (Please, we're begging you)

....

Guests

I'm so happy you're having a baby and I'm not!

....

Um...Now what do we do?

....

....

Wishes For The Lil Poop Factory

....

....

Baby's First Swear Word

....

....

Who will hit the bottle first?

....

....

Willing to babysit? (Please, we're begging you)

....

Guests

I'm so happy you're having a baby and I'm not!

....

Um...Now what do we do?

....

....

Wishes For The Lil Poop Factory

....

....

Baby's First Swear Word

....

Who will hit the bottle first?

....

Willing to babysit? (Please, we're begging you)

....

Guests

I'm so happy you're having a baby and I'm not!

....

Um...Now what do we do?

....

....

Wishes For The Lil Poop Factory

....

....

Baby's First Swear Word

....

....

Who will hit the bottle first?

....

....

Willing to babysit? (Please, we're begging you)

....

Guests

I'm so happy you're having a baby and I'm not!

....

Um...Now what do we do?

....

....

Wishes For The Lil Poop Factory

....

....

Baby's First Swear Word

....

Who will hit the bottle first?

....

Willing to babysit? (Please, we're begging you)

....

Guests

I'm so happy you're having a baby and I'm not!

....

Um...Now what do we do?

....

....

Wishes For The Lil Poop Factory

....

....

Baby's First Swear Word

....

Who will hit the bottle first?

....

Willing to babysit? (Please, we're begging you)

....

Guests

I'm so happy you're having a baby and I'm not!

....

Um...Now what do we do?

....

....

Wishes For The Lil Poop Factory

....

....

Baby's First Swear Word

....

Who will hit the bottle first?

....

Willing to babysit? (Please, we're begging you)

....

Guests

I'm so happy you're having a baby and I'm not!

....

Um...Now what do we do?

....

....

Wishes For The Lil Poop Factory

....

....

Baby's First Swear Word

....

Who will hit the bottle first?

....

Willing to babysit? (Please, we're begging you)

....

Guests

I'm so happy you're having a baby and I'm not!

....

Um...Now what do we do?

....

....

Wishes For The Lil Poop Factory

....

....

Baby's First Swear Word

....

Who will hit the bottle first?

....

Willing to babysit? (Please, we're begging you)

....

Guests

I'm so happy you're having a baby and I'm not!

....

Um...Now what do we do?

....

....

Wishes For The Lil Poop Factory

....

....

Baby's First Swear Word

....

Who will hit the bottle first?

....

Willing to babysit? (Please, we're begging you)

....

Guests

I'm so happy you're having a baby and I'm not!

....

Um...Now what do we do?

....

....

Wishes For The Lil Poop Factory

....

....

Baby's First Swear Word

....

Who will hit the bottle first?

....

Willing to babysit? (Please, we're begging you)

....

Guests

I'm so happy you're having a baby and I'm not!

....

Um...Now what do we do?

....

....

Wishes For The Lil Poop Factory

....

....

Baby's First Swear Word

....

Who will hit the bottle first?

....

Willing to babysit? (Please, we're begging you)

....

Guests

I'm so happy you're having a baby and I'm not!

....

Um...Now what do we do?

....

....

Wishes For The Lil Poop Factory

....

....

Baby's First Swear Word

....

Who will hit the bottle first?

....

Willing to babysit? (Please, we're begging you)

....

Guests

I'm so happy you're having a baby and I'm not!

....

Um...Now what do we do?

....

....

Wishes For The Lil Poop Factory

....

....

Baby's First Swear Word

....

Who will hit the bottle first?

....

Willing to babysit? (Please, we're begging you)

....

Guests

I'm so happy you're having a baby and I'm not!

....

Um...Now what do we do?

....

....

Wishes For The Lil Poop Factory

....

....

Baby's First Swear Word

....

Who will hit the bottle first?

....

Willing to babysit? (Please, we're begging you)

....

Guests

I'm so happy you're having a baby and I'm not!

....

Um...Now what do we do?

....

....

Wishes For The Lil Poop Factory

....

....

Baby's First Swear Word

....

Who will hit the bottle first?

....

Willing to babysit? (Please, we're begging you)

....

Guests

I'm so happy you're having a baby and I'm not!

....

Um...Now what do we do?

....

....

Wishes For The Lil Poop Factory

....

....

Baby's First Swear Word

....

Who will hit the bottle first?

....

Willing to babysit? (Please, we're begging you)

....

Guests

I'm so happy you're having a baby and I'm not!

....

Um...Now what do we do?

....

....

Wishes For The Lil Poop Factory

....

....

Baby's First Swear Word

....

Who will hit the bottle first?

....

Willing to babysit? (Please, we're begging you)

....

Guests

I'm so happy you're having a baby and I'm not!

....

Um...Now what do we do?

....

....

Wishes For The Lil Poop Factory

....

....

Baby's First Swear Word

....

....

Who will hit the bottle first?

....

Willing to babysit? (Please, we're begging you)

....

Guests

I'm so happy you're having a baby and I'm not!

....

Um...Now what do we do?

....

....

Wishes For The Lil Poop Factory

....

....

Baby's First Swear Word

....

Who will hit the bottle first?

....

Willing to babysit? (Please, we're begging you)

....

Guests

I'm so happy you're having a baby and I'm not!

....

Um...Now what do we do?

....

....

Wishes For The Lil Poop Factory

....

....

Baby's First Swear Word

....

Who will hit the bottle first?

....

Willing to babysit? (Please, we're begging you)

....

Guests

I'm so happy you're having a baby and I'm not!

....

Um...Now what do we do?

....

....

Wishes For The Lil Poop Factory

....

....

Baby's First Swear Word

....

Who will hit the bottle first?

....

Willing to babysit? (Please, we're begging you)

....

Guests

I'm so happy you're having a baby and I'm not!

....

Um...Now what do we do?

....

....

Wishes For The Lil Poop Factory

....

....

Baby's First Swear Word

....

Who will hit the bottle first?

....

Willing to babysit? (Please, we're begging you)

....

Guests

I'm so happy you're having a baby and I'm not!

....

Um...Now what do we do?

....

....

Wishes For The Lil Poop Factory

....

....

Baby's First Swear Word

....

Who will hit the bottle first?

....

Willing to babysit? (Please, we're begging you)

....

Guests

I'm so happy you're having a baby and I'm not!

....

Um...Now what do we do?

....

....

Wishes For The Lil Poop Factory

....

....

Baby's First Swear Word

....

Who will hit the bottle first?

....

Willing to babysit? (Please, we're begging you)

....

Guests

I'm so happy you're having a baby and I'm not!

....

Um...Now what do we do?

....

....

Wishes For The Lil Poop Factory

....

....

Baby's First Swear Word

....

....

Who will hit the bottle first?

....

Willing to babysit? (Please, we're begging you)

....

Guests

I'm so happy you're having a baby and I'm not!

....

Um...Now what do we do?

....

....

Wishes For The Lil Poop Factory

....

....

Baby's First Swear Word

....

....

Who will hit the bottle first?

....

....

Willing to babysit? (Please, we're begging you)

....

Guests

I'm so happy you're having a baby and I'm not!

....

Um...Now what do we do?

....

....

Wishes For The Lil Poop Factory

....

....

Baby's First Swear Word

....

....

Who will hit the bottle first?

....

Willing to babysit? (Please, we're begging you)

....

Guests

I'm so happy you're having a baby and I'm not!

....

Um...Now what do we do?

....

....

Wishes For The Lil Poop Factory

....

....

Baby's First Swear Word

....

Who will hit the bottle first?

....

Willing to babysit? (Please, we're begging you)

....

Guests

I'm so happy you're having a baby and I'm not!

....

Um...Now what do we do?

....

....

Wishes For The Lil Poop Factory

....

....

Baby's First Swear Word

....

Who will hit the bottle first?

....

Willing to babysit? (Please, we're begging you)

....

Guests

I'm so happy you're having a baby and I'm not!

....

Um...Now what do we do?

....

....

Wishes For The Lil Poop Factory

....

....

Baby's First Swear Word

....

Who will hit the bottle first?

....

Willing to babysit? (Please, we're begging you)

....

Guests

I'm so happy you're having a baby and I'm not!

....

Um...Now what do we do?

....

....

Wishes For The Lil Poop Factory

....

....

Baby's First Swear Word

....

....

Who will hit the bottle first?

....

Willing to babysit? (Please, we're begging you)

....

Guests

I'm so happy you're having a baby and I'm not!

....

Um...Now what do we do?

....

....

Wishes For The Lil Poop Factory

....

....

Baby's First Swear Word

....

Who will hit the bottle first?

....

Willing to babysit? (Please, we're begging you)

....

Memories

Memories

Memories

Memories

Memories

Memories

Memories

Memories

Memories

Memories

Made in United States
Troutdale, OR
02/27/2025

29318861R00066